Zen and the Art of Drumming

by

Russ Frost

The Osoba Publishing Company

Columbus, Ohio

©2012

Zen and the Art of Drumming
By Russ Frost
©2012

ISBN: 978-0-578-10788-2

Cover Design by Ian Russell Frost Designs
San Diego, California

Photography by Howard Rosenzweig
contact via author

Russ Frost
www.russfrost.com

This book is dedicated to two very special people. They have shown me how to age with dignity and grace. They have given me the foundation for helping to build a sense of family. They have taught me the meaning of how to give and help others. Their love and caring has helped me become the person I am today. They are my in-laws: James "Hob" Neff and Sally Neff. I could never thank them enough for everything I have received from them.

Zen and the Art of Drumming will elicit thought, introspection and enlightenment as related to drummers and drumming.

Zen and the Art of Drumming combines sayings just as they are, sayings with anecdotes, and inspiring Zen and drum illustrations. Whether one is a seasoned veteran drummer or just starting out you will be able to enjoy this book. Many of the sayings will help put one's drumming journey in perspective.

As much as this book is focused on drums and drumming other musicians can benefit as well. It is my hope that this book helps you on your journey and adventure into the world of drums and drumming.

Success, real success, in any endeavor, demands more from an individual than most people are willing to offer – not more than they are capable of offering.

James Roche

Do not expect anything original from an echo. Unknown

Band members for a local band are over at their friend's house just hanging around.

"We're a cover band, *Dude*. We get one to three gigs a week, and we're doin' pretty good," says the guitar player in a proud tone.

"Yeah, we're in the studio now trying to put together a CD," adds the drummer, confirming the band's direction.

"Gonna send it to some record companies?" asks their friend.

"*Dude*, we're a pretty tight band," says the bass player bragging.

"Got any originals?" questions the friend.

"No, *Dude*, we're just taking ten songs we already play on gigs," the guitar player says with pride.

"Oh . . . good luck," says the friend sarcastically.

The way to bring out the best in you is not by chance. It is by preparation.

Unknown

Always bear in mind that your own resolution to succeed is more important than any one thing. A. Lincoln

I don't have a lot of talent. I've seen young drummers with talent, and they make it look so easy. It's never been easy for me. I work on my drumming almost every day. I read about drumming, listen to other drummers, go on-line to watch drummers on YouTube, and take lessons.

I've gone out and played drum circles, open jams, open stages and played with friends. I've formed several groups and played coffee cafes, bars, private parties, retirement centers, festivals, corporate events, and any place that would have me.

I still don't have much talent, however, I feel I can play with anyone and in any venue. So, I call myself a drummer.

I think every band is a little cautious when the drummer starts to write tunes.

Matt Cameron

A good teacher has been defined as one who makes himself progressively unnecessary. Unknown

My student, Jeff, has been studying with me for a couple of years. He practices and always comes ready to learn. He has been going to open stage nights to sit in with other musicians. Some friends of his are musicians, and they get together on a regular basis to play.

One day Jeff shows up, and we start our lesson. About ten minutes into the lesson we have a pause in playing, and he asks me a question.

"How long do you think I need to take lessons?"

"Why do you ask?" I respond with curiosity.

"You've been a great teacher, and I've learned a lot. I still learn from you, however, I'm also learning from other drummers. I can watch how and what they play and understand it," he states.

"You've grown a lot, Jeff. When you started you had trouble coordinating your hands and feet. You've worked hard, and now it's second nature."

"That's because you're a good teacher."

"Thank you, although I have to say that even a good teacher needs a good student."

"I feel comfortable playing. I know there's still plenty to learn though," explains Jeff.

"Never stop learning. You will change over time, and your music will change as well. I am proud of you, Jeff. Going on your own to play music is a compliment to me as your teacher. It says we both have done our part to get you to this independent point."

"You are not mad that I'd be stopping?" Jeff asks.

"Absolutely not," I say.

"If I need something…"

"I'll always make time for you. It's been a pleasure to be your teacher," I offer and then continue with, "Let's finish up this lesson. I've got a couple of cold beers with our names on them to celebrate."

A wise man will make more
opportunity than he finds.

F. Bacon

If you understand, things are just as they are; if you do not understand, things are just as they are.

Zen Saying

Lengthen Your Line. E. Parker

I've been practicing with a couple of other drummers. One is a tall, strongly built guy with a warm smile. He's very good. The other guy is also good even though he is much younger and seems to have more talent than patience.

Out of the three of us I feel I am the least competent. I told my teacher, Eric, about my feelings of maybe being inadequate to play with these guys. Eric, a veteran teacher, listened carefully and then asked if I had some chalk. I did have some sidewalk chalk.

We walked outside and on the driveway he drew a line about two feet long.

Eric then asked, "How can you make this line shorter?"

I thought of erasing some of it although I knew that seemed too obvious.

"I'm not sure," I said after some thought.

Eric leaned down and drew a line about three feet long. "Now, it's shorter. . . Improve yourself, and don't worry about others," he instructed before adding, "think about it."

So, for the next several months I practiced and played with whomever I could find. When the three of us got together again I felt I held my own.

"*Man*, nice job. You've been practicing," said the tall drummer as he smiled that infectious smile.

I couldn't have received a better compliment.

That which we persist in doing becomes easier – not that the nature of the task has changed, but our ability to do it has increased.

Emerson

In risk there is opportunity. Unknown

A drum student is talking to his teacher.

"I've been practicing every day, yet when I gig I don't think I sound as good as when I practice," the student comments to his teacher.

"Whenever we play in front of an audience, be it one or a thousand times, we are judged. That can add stress and tension to your playing and alter it," responds the teacher.

"I know I can play so much better, but I pull back."

"During practice imagine there are always people there listening to you play. As you play always try to play your best. When it's time for a gig you will have already risked your best. When it comes to a gig it won't be the first time you have risked playing your best. It will be an opportunity to play and enjoy yourself being at your best," offers the teacher.

Maximum capabilities are directly proportionate to the time and effort you are willing to give it.

L. Moorehouse

It's the space between the notes. Unknown

Young Drummer to Old Drummer

"Did you check my solo out last night?" asks the boasting young drummer.

"I heard it," the old drummer replies.

"Pretty awesome, huh?" the young drummer says expecting confirmation from the veteran drummer.

"Well, you play fast and have some talent, but…" the old drummer says before hesitating.

"But, WHAT?" demands the young drummer, as if there was any room for buts.

"You didn't let your solo breathe. It was kind of like a run on sentence," the old drummer says with a constructive tone.

"*Man*, I thought I killed it," reflects the young drummer.

"You did kill it; now, let's bury it," states the old drummer.

"What are you talkin' 'bout?" the young drummer asks peeved to hear anything other than confirmation of his greatness.

"Soloing is about telling a story. It's not just the notes and how fast you play them but what's between those notes. Understand the space between notes and you go from good to great," instructs the old drummer.

"So, maybe less is more?" the young drummer inquires.

"Now you're getting it!" responds the old drummer.

Even if you are on the right track, you get run over if you just sit there.

W. Rodgers

Things do not happen in the world, they are brought about. W. Hayes

After a tryout with a local band

"Yeah, *Man*, I'd like to join," the bass player says as he initiates his prerogative before asking, "So, who do we have then?"

"We got bass, guitar, keys and yours truly on the drums," responds the drummer.

"So, how many times a week do we practice?" the bass player questions.

"Twice, sometimes three times if no one is gigging with their other bands," informs the drummer.

Seemingly confused by the direction of the drummer's banter, the bass player does not betray himself by asking, "That's great, but do you have any gigs coming up?"

"No, *Man*, WE need to get on that," the guitar player interjects.

"Who's been doing the contacting, website, fliers, Facebook, contracts and such?" the bass player asks, again staying true to his inquisitive nature.

"We're gonna be a killer band!" predicts the keys player.

"I can see that, but who gets the gigs?"

"We all do," the drummer says wanting to make an impact on the new member the importance of everyone contributing.

Two months later at rehearsal

"*Man*, we only got ten songs," the guitar player begins.

"What other songs do you want to learn?" asks the bass player.

"I dunno, *Man*, whatever," the guitar player replies with his head down as if a great potential will become unfulfilled.

"Have any of you contacted any clubs or places for us to play?" the bass player asks.

"No."

"No."

"No."

"My cousin knows this dude who might get us an opening gig. I'm waiting for him to call me back," the drummer remarks.

"I gotta tell you that I think I'm dropping out," the bass player stunningly quips.

"What?"

"Why?"

"How come, *Dude?*"

"Well, I don't want to do everything myself and you guys don't seem motivated to make this happen," concludes the irony-challenged bassist.

"*Man*, you'll regret it!" the guitar player predicts.

"*Man*, I already do," reflects the bass player.

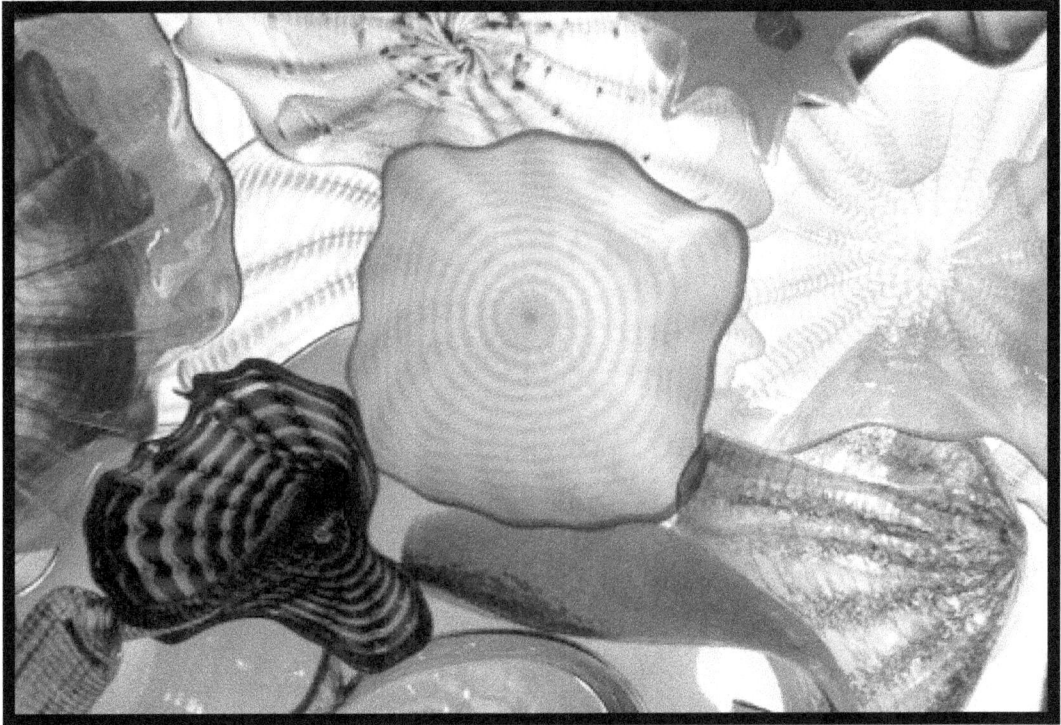

Without music to decorate it, time is just a bunch of boring production deadlines or dates by which bills must be paid.

Frank Zappa

Use what talents you possess. The woods would be very silent if no birds sang there except those that sang best. H. Van Dyke

Cheryl was a very attractive woman about forty-two years old. She had long brown hair and beautiful blue eyes. She stood about five feet two inches but seemed taller once you had met her. Her dynamic personality gave the impression of a woman with confidence.

The first time I saw her she was playing the drum set with a three piece jazz band. They were alright, however, the trio sounded as if they needed more practice time together. They just weren't locked in.

At the set break I walked up to Cheryl and introduced myself. I told her I was a drummer, too. We sat and talked some before I asked this question, "How often do you guys get together?"

"At least once a week or sometimes twice if there's time," Cheryl responded while looking at me with her big smile as if she knew what I was thinking…and she did. Cheryl continued, "I'm not that good. I practice and maybe I could practice more, but it's tough to find the time. I've got a full time job and three kids," she informed me before taking a deep breath then exhaling slowly. "I wish I was better you know, more talent and time to practice. I love playing this music. You're getting the best we have with what we got," she stated as she slightly tilted her head to the side waiting for my response.

"Your trio sounds good. I'm glad I got to see you perform," I said with a new understanding that it's about the music and the love of playing.

"Stick around for the next set. I sing a little and if that doesn't scare you…" she said as she laughed, got up, and walked back to the stage.

Even though we take different roads to ascend the wooden mountain, each of us can achieve our goal and appreciate the moon when we reach the top.

Chinese Folk Song

It's more probable that your attitude, rather than your aptitude, will determine your altitude in life.

Dan Zadra

A ship in harbor is safe but that's not what ships are for. J. Shedd

Two friends are sitting on a porch during a warm spring evening. As they sit watching some neighborhood kids run up the street, one drummer friend with no gig experience confides to the other.

"I'm afraid."

"*Dude*, you've been in that basement way too long."

"I know, but what if I screw up?"

"You wanted to become a drummer. Now, you know how to play except you got to take it out there. That's what you have been practicing for."

"I know we all have to get that first gig under our belt. I'm still scared to death."

"Understood, but it's time to get those drums out of the basement and launch yourself."

"Nice play on words."

"This gig today is a small one, but a great way to get your feet wet."

"Calm seas, eh?"

"Best way to start."

"Thanks."

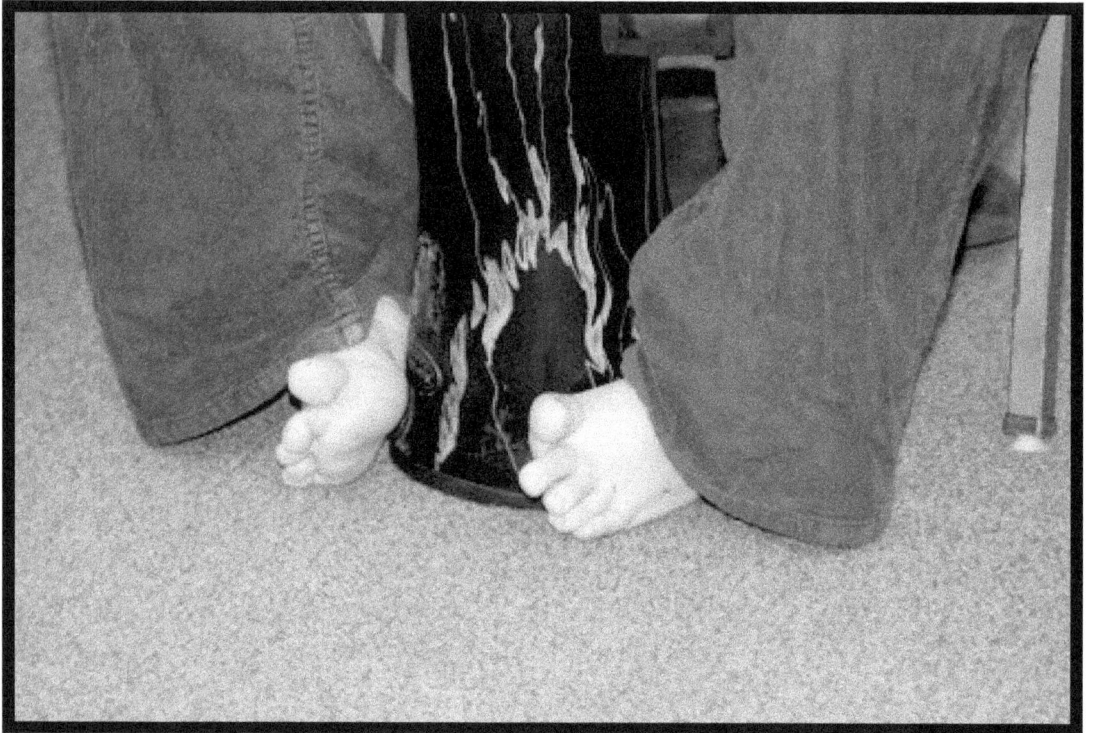

I shall be telling this with a sigh
somewhere ages and ages hence.
Two roads diverged in a wood,
and I – I took the one less traveled
by, and that has made all the
difference.

R. Frost

You've removed most of the roadblocks to success when you've learned the difference between motion and direction.

B. Copeland

A couple of drummer friends, get together to have a drink at their favorite bar.

"*Man*, I'm playin' all over. I've been hitting all the open stages."

"That's cool, *Dude*, but what's your goal?"

"Goal?"

"Yeah, goal. What do you want to do, or where do you want to take your music?"

"Man, I don't know. Just play I guess?"

"Oh, I've always wanted to play on a big stage with a kick ass band, and I'm just layin' down some hardcore grooves."

"Yeah, me too!"

"Really?"

Practice what you know and it will help to make clear what now you do not know.

R. Van Rijn

If you aren't in complete control of a situation anything you do can make it worse. H. Leary

The band breaks after the first set at a night club. The band leader comes right up to the drummer.

"What the hell happened?"

"My bad!"

"You totally lost it right in the middle."

"Uh . . . yeah . . . well, I tried to play some triplets over four."

"You missed."

"Guess I need to practice that before doing it again."

"You think? How about you try it in rehearsal first?"

"Uh...alright."

If you do not change direction, you may end up where you are heading.

Lao Tzu

If the only tool you have is a hammer you tend to see every problem as a nail.

A. Maslow

"*Man*, is that the only beat you know?"

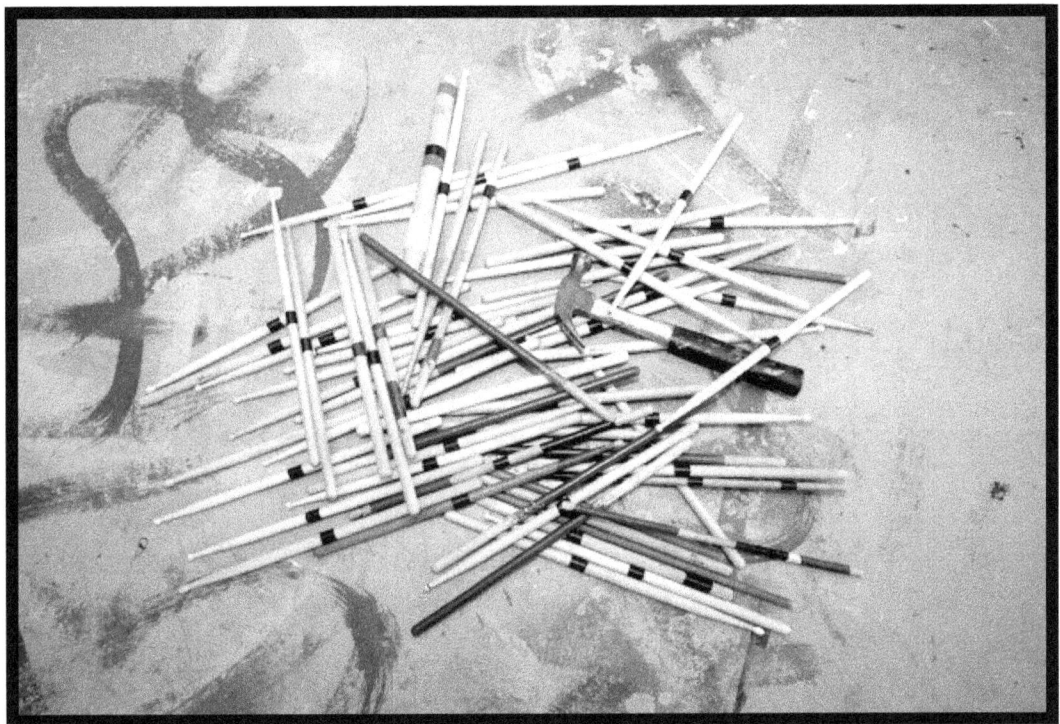

Everything has two handles, by one of which it ought to be carried and by the other not.

Epictetus

When I let go of what I am, I become what I might be.

Lao Tzu

No one cares to speak to an unwilling listener. An arrow never lodges in a stone, often it recoils upon the sender of it.

St. Jerome

One of my students, Leon, asks if I would be interested in having another student, and of course I say, "Yes."

"He's kinda stubborn," Leon offers.

"What do you mean, stubborn?" I ask.

"He's a know–it–all kinda guy. He likes people to think he already knows things."

"Ok, thanks for the heads up," I say.

I get a call from Leon's friend Danny, and we arrange a lesson.

"Hi, Danny, tell me about what you know and can play." I state.

"I've been playin' awhile. I just pick stuff up here and there and watch other drummers."

"Why do you want to take lessons?" I question.

"Leon says you're cool so I thought, why not?"

"Alright, let's begin. Play me a jazz groove if you know one," I command.

"I know," he says, then plays something I can't quite grasp, that doesn't have a jazz feel at all.

"Interesting, what would you play for a rock song?"

"I know," Danny says again before playing something that I'm not sure what it is.

"Let's start here with the rock beat. Try playing this," I demo a beat as Danny shakes his head affirmatively.

"I know," he says before playing something similar to what he played before. Afterwards he says, "You know I play in a couple bands. Everyone says they love my playing."

I think for a few moments then make a decision. "Danny, I'm not sure I'm the right teacher for you. Maybe it's best if we not continue," I offer.

"Cool," he says and then follows with the ever ready, "I know."

Few things help an individual more than to place responsibility upon him and to let him know that you trust him.

B. Washington

My chief want in life is someone who shall make me do what I can. R. W. Emerson

I'm a pusher. Always have been and every now and then I am reminded why I need to stay this way. I've played drums professionally for a lot of years. I've played with some of the best musicians around. I've toured several times, and I know what it takes to get to that level.

Andy came to me having been self-taught for a year. I saw right away he had talent. It took some time to get him to make changes and even more time to do what I told him to do. You see, Andy was lazy . . . talented but lazy. That angered me. It's one thing to be lazy with no talent and quite another to have talent and let it go to waste. I know I made Andy mad many times as I pushed him to work on his skills. He even stopped coming to lessons for a time.

After three years Andy's family moved away, and I lost touch with him.

It was five years later that I got a postcard from Andy. "Check this out," was all he said along with a listed website.

I pulled up the website and recognized the band. It was a band I heard was the newest, hottest band on the east coast. I even heard how tight they were, and the guys could really play. Right there in the middle of the band's photo was Andy. He somehow looked more mature and confident.

About a week later I got another postcard from Andy, "Thanks for pushing me. I couldn't have done it without you. Andy."

That's why I won't change!

Most people do not listen with the intent to understand;
They listen with the intent to reply.

S. Covey

To Avoid Criticism do nothing, say nothing, be nothing. E. Hubbard

"He said I didn't play very well."

"Was he right?"

"I don't know, maybe."

"If you perform, compete, work, or breathe you are open for criticism."

"What should I do?"

"Perform, compete, work and definitely breathe."

Men who know the same things are not long the best company for each other.

Emerson

Who knows useful things, not many things, is wise. Aeschylus

Two drummers strike a conversation at a PASIC conference.

"Man, I can play jazz, rock, blues, salsa, rhythm and blues, reggae, calypso, and Afro-Cuban."

"Where do you live?"

"The South!"

"What do you usually play?"

"Country, I play country just about all the time."

Always do your best. What you plant now, you will harvest later.

Og Mandino

Before strongly desiring anything, we should look carefully into the happiness of its present owner.
La Rochefoucauld

Two drummers are sitting around a friend's computer watching a YouTube of their favorite band.

"I wish I could be just like him."

"Why? He's got three ex-wives, five kids, four DUIs, been to rehab three times, lost most of his money, arrested countless times, and been kicked out of more bands than we've even played in."

"Oh, I guess I mean drum as well as he can."

There is a time to let things happen and a time to make things happen.

H. Prathar

Be not afraid of growing slowly; be afraid only of standing still. Unknown

"Hey, how've you been?" asks drummer number one to a friend of his.

"Not bad, and you?" drummer number two echos.

"Good. You playin' any place?" drummer number one inquires.

"Wherever I can, but it's tough to find gigs right now. I'm still working on things, and every chance I get I try and play out," drummer number two states a little dejected then continues, "You?"

"Nah, just stopped the gig thing, and it's been tough getting the other guys together," sighs drummer number one.

"I thought you were working more on jazz," states drummer number two.

"I was and still need to," drummer number one confirms.

"Don't wait on others," drummer number two reminds.

"Yeah, I know," comes back the acknowledgement.

Before enlightenment I chopped wood and carried water. After enlightenment I chopped wood and carried water. Unknown

"Here's how you play this," the teacher instructs his student as they sit in the small rehearsal space facing each other.

"Wow, it seems difficult even when I think I play it right," the student responds with curiosity that his abilities aren't matching up with the feel of the groove.

"Practice, practice and more practice. The more practice the better it will feel," the teacher comments to the student observing his impatience.

"Will I play it better then?" the student asks.

"No, you will just be better," confirms the teacher.

Joe's been my drummer for 14 years and we've been buddies for six. . .

John Mayall

Balance mind, body, and soul. Unknown

High school band was the best. Marching at football games and then basketball season rolls around, our team was good, and we were rockin' the house from the stands.

After high school my drums sat in the basement as I focused on college. Occasionally, I would sit and play, although not for very long.

I graduated from college, moved away, and was lucky to find a job with a good company. I went to work, came home, worked out, dated some and stayed busy. Something was missing, though, as I moved through life as a young adult. My apartment was in a very hip part of town, but something was missing. The girls I dated were all nice, but something was missing.

In the fall I returned home to visit my mom. She asked if I would go downstairs and bring up some extra chairs. That's when everything changed. As I turned on the lights and walked downstairs my old drum set sat there as it had for years. The light glistened off the chrome as the cymbals still held their tilted angle that I liked. I stopped, remembering all the incredible times I had playing my drums and how I looked forward to drumming.

That's the missing piece I thought. Drumming had become part of my soul and having neglected it for so long I was experiencing its loss in my current life.

I sat on my old throne that was worn with loose seams and a depressed cushion, picked up my beaten, dented, and worn drum sticks and started with a simple beat. It was like giving water to a thirsty man. I sat up, found an old groove, and played. They say you have a mind, body, and soul; all three need to be in balance. Today I found that missing piece. I fed my soul with the drumming of my youth, and I started back on my journey of balancing mind, body, and soul.

You exist to serve the music. The music does not exist to serve you!

Jamie Muir

The difference between a successful person and others is not a lack of strength, not a lack of knowledge, but rather a lack in will.

Vince Lombardi

There is only one success – to be able to spend your life in your own way. C. Morley

"It's just a job. It pays the bills, but I live to drum," he says as if stating a life philosophy to a friend.

"Are you happy?" She asks.

"Sometimes."

"What about changing your life?" She inquires trying to dig a little deeper.

"How so?"

"What about drumming to live? Make drumming your life instead of just a small part," she offers as if opening a new chapter in a book.

"I need to eat, pay the rent and car payments," he counters.

"OK, but… you can teach drumming, gig, do workshops, write, sell and share your love of drumming," she summarizes.

"That's a lot to think about."

"What's happiness worth?"

"You've got a point."

If at first you don't succeed, try, try again. Then quit. There's no use being a damn fool about it.

W.C. Fields

The greatest mistake you can make in life is to continually be afraid you will make one.

Unknown

The rehearsal finishes and the band is just hanging around breaking down their gear.

"We're going into the studio this Friday," reminds the band leader.

"Yeah, I'm a little nervous," the new drummer states.

"About?"

"Screwing up!"

"It's the studio, *Dude.* You just do another take," the band leader interjects trying to put things in perspective.

"Yeah I know, yet I still don't want to screw up."

"Then here's what you do. On the first song of the first take deliberately mess up," commands the leader.

"Why would I do that?"

"To get it out of your system. You'll see there's nothing to be afraid of, and we'll just do another take."

"Are you sure?"

"Everyone screws up at some point, even the greats. You're a good drummer. Get the fear out of you then move on."

"I'll give it a try."

Art does not make the man; man makes the art.

G. Funakoshi

You will never find time for anything. If you want time, you must make it. Unknown

Question:

How can you find the time to practice, if... you have a job, family and other obligations in your life?

Answer:

Make a list of what you need to do today. Take care of these things first. Then make a list of what you want to do and prioritize the list. If drumming is important for you, then schedule it high on the list. Don't hope it happens; make it happen.

If a man does not keep pace with his companions, perhaps it is because he hears a different drummer. Let him step to the music which he hears, however measured or far away.

H. D. Thoreau

Nothing can stop the man with the right mental attitude from achieving his goal; nothing on earth can help the man with the wrong mental attitude. T. Jefferson

Two best friends:

"I can't do it. It's just too hard!"

"Then quit!"

"What? Shouldn't you be encouraging me?"

"I would normally, but you won't get it."

"Why not?"

"Cuz, you think you can't."

Doing more things faster is no substitute for doing the right thing.

S. Covey

The next best thing to knowing something is knowing where to find it. Unknown

"How'd you know that?"

"Teacher

YouTube

Internet

Public Library

CD

DVD

Books

Drummer Friend

TV

School

Workshop

Conference

My mom told me."

Where there's no gardener,
there's no garden.

Unknown

Nothing ever exists entirely alone; everything is in relation to everything else.

Unknown

Yesterday I was invited to attend a drum circle that was held in a beautiful park near downtown. There were picnic tables in the area with some pine trees outlining an open section. The sun was shining as cotton ball puffs of clouds strolled by. Every week, during warmer weather, this drum circle has met. It has done this for several years with a lot of the same participants.

As I approached there were about twenty people sitting in a circle with various types of hand drums. One person had an African djun djun drum on a stand. At some point she started a base rhythm beat. I took a seat in the circle with my conga drum and thought I would listen first. Slowly people started to join in, and before long everyone but myself was playing something.

I leaned back in my chair and tried to discern the groove. It was difficult. I looked at the participants with some having their heads down totally into what they were doing while others were looking around as if in search of something. Several played with smiles on their face seemingly enjoying the overall experience.

I then started to play, unsure what I was contributing, but trying to relate to the djun djun drum. I thought that with a little understanding this could be a really great thing to experience. If only everyone would listen and understand that working together would enhance our group dynamics. After playing for about ten minutes and wondering how quickly I could leave without appearing disrespectful a middle aged man approached, smiled and stood by the side of the circle until the group ceased playing. Most in the group noticed him and greeted him warmly. He entered the circle like a lion tamer enters a ring. He walked over to the djun djun drummer and sang a beat propelling the djun djun drummer to start to play that beat. He then went around and dissected the circle giving each part a certain beat. All, including myself, followed his lead.

I was amazed at how the groove locked in. Now, everyone was looking at everyone else as if acknowledging their contribution. The circle felt powerful, dynamic, and alive. The parts became a whole as we all became interconnected.

The best way to make your dreams come true is to wake up.

Paul Valery

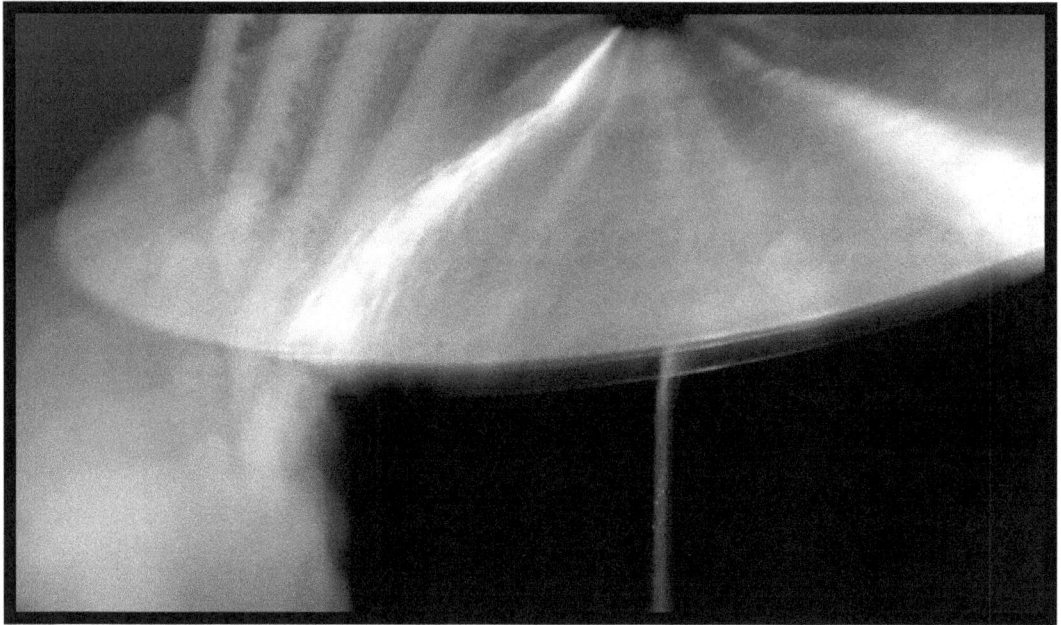

Man is the product of his thoughts. What he thinks, he becomes. Unknown

Some musicians are standing around a bar when a drummer comes over with a dejected look on his face.

"What's wrong?"

"I haven't been keeping time very well. I increase the tempo as the song progresses. I suck! I get lost sometimes and miss changes. I don't like the music. I don't feel comfortable playing with these guys. I keep changing my set-up cuz it doesn't seem right. I don't think they like me. If only I lost some weight I might play stronger."

"Hey Nathan, is this guy any good?" yells one musician over to another.

"Nope...he sucks!"

Don't argue with idiots. They will bring you down to their level and beat you with experience.

Unknown

Act as if what you do makes a difference. It does. W. James

I love the congas. I've played and have been involved in making drums for over twenty years. Some guys called and asked if I would come and sit in with them. They were opening up for another band and played for only one hour. Of course I said yes before they reminded me there's no money.

I showed up early and waited until I was told we could set up. The sound man gave me one mic. I do believe most sound guys have hearing problems. When we started to play I could barely hear my congas. I asked for a couple of adjustments with the stage monitor then, thought the hell with it. I'll just play through the sound and do the best I can. The band played and it felt like the volume alone was rocking the house. I didn't think anyone could even hear me so I backed off a little.

To my amazement when our hour was up many people came up and said I sounded great. Even the band members said I added a piece that made the whole band better. I was invited back and played every week until the bar changed ownership and direction.

Who'd a thought it!

All that is gold does not glitter;
not all those that wander are lost.

Tolkien

94

It takes a wise man to learn from his mistakes, but an even wiser man to learn from others.

Zen Proverb

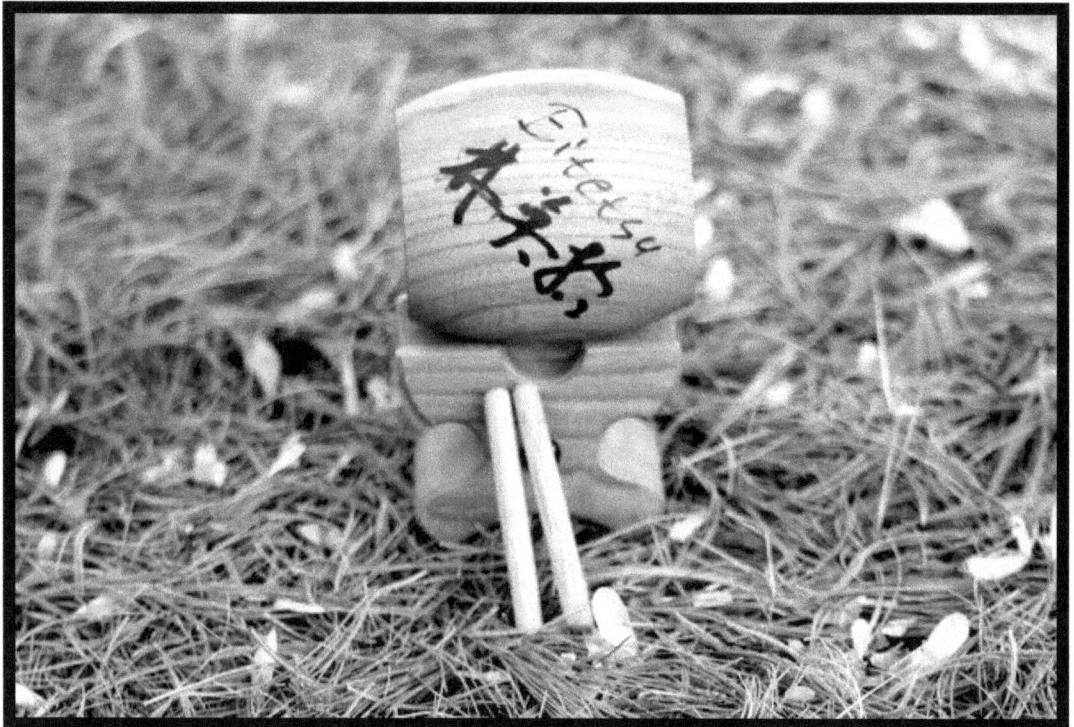

I have no special talent. I am only passionately curious. A. Einstein

I got a call the other day from a bass player I know. He asked if I was interested in a new band he was putting together. I was, however, I also knew I was spread pretty thin so I thanked him and then declined. He asked if I knew any other drummers. One of my oldest students came to mind. He started with me over ten years ago. When he started I thought he would never last. His rhythm fluctuated, his coordination was questionable, and his tempo was all over the place. He said he had dreamed of playing drums all his life but only now has the money and time to pursue it.

What this guy lacked in talent he made up for in commitment. Over time he worked hard on his weaknesses. Years later I've seen him playing in several bands. He won't blow you away, nevertheless, he'll give you a solid pocket. He will also do something a lot of drummers often forget to do; he will play with passion that resonates through the whole band.

"Here, call this guy. If you're lucky to get him, he'll do a great job," I said proudly as I passed on the contact information.

"Thanks, *Man*."

"My pleasure."

Go confidently in the direction of your dreams. Live the life you have imagined.

H. D. Thoreau

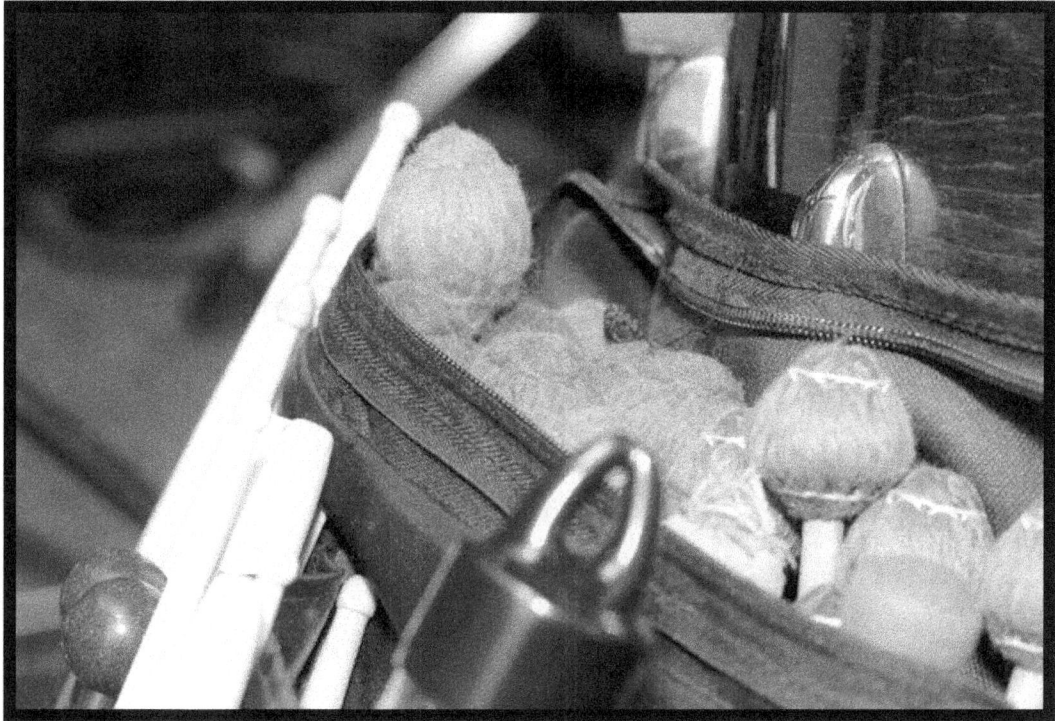

A man cannot be comfortable without his own approval. M. Twain

Two musicians who are acquaintances are sitting around drinking coffee the day after a gig:

"I don't like the way I'm playing. My fills seem off, timing fluctuates, I missed going into a bridge, I wanted to re-tune my drums as soon as I started playing. Do you think I sounded any good?"

"Why should I, if you don't?"

If you think you stink,

you probably do.

Buddy Rich

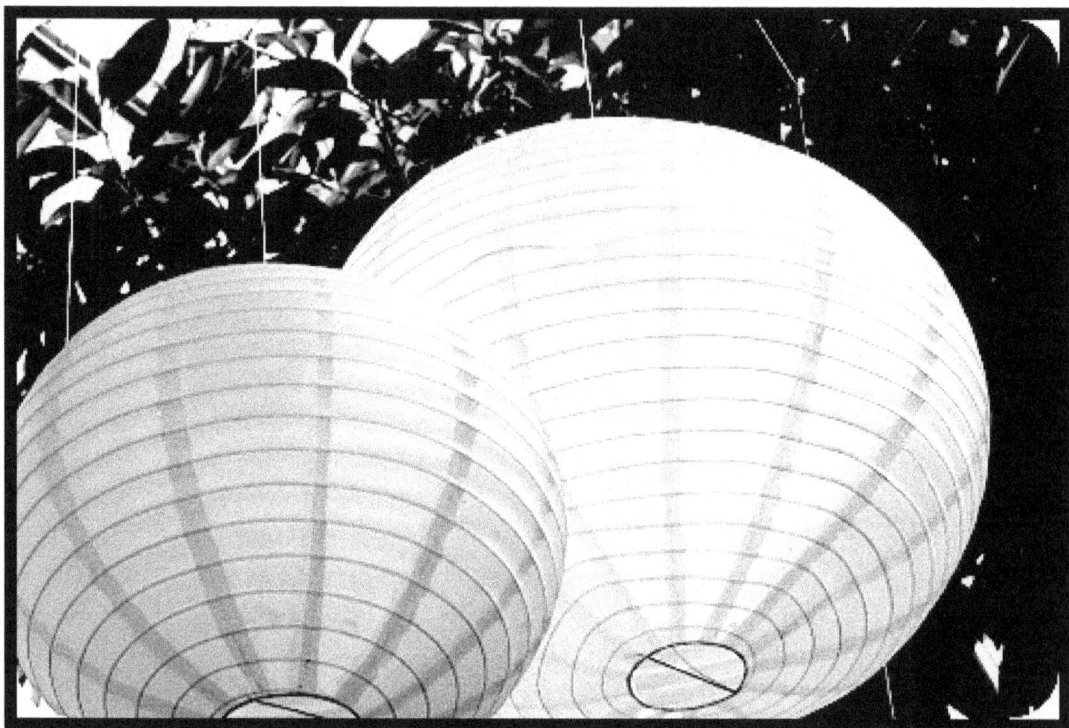

Information is not knowledge.

Albert Einstein

Do not dwell in the past, do not dream of the future, concentrate the mind on the present. Buddha

One musician talking to his friend about another musician:

"Man, I had problems with him before. He plays great, but I don't know."

"Have you talked to him?"

"Not yet. We're hoping to tour some next summer, in spite of this, I don't know if it will work."

"Maybe now is the time to take care of business and your issues with him."

"Now?"

"How about right now? Talk to him and deal with it now. Later might take care of itself."

"Ya think?"

Nothing in life is to be feared. It is only to be understood.

Marie Curie

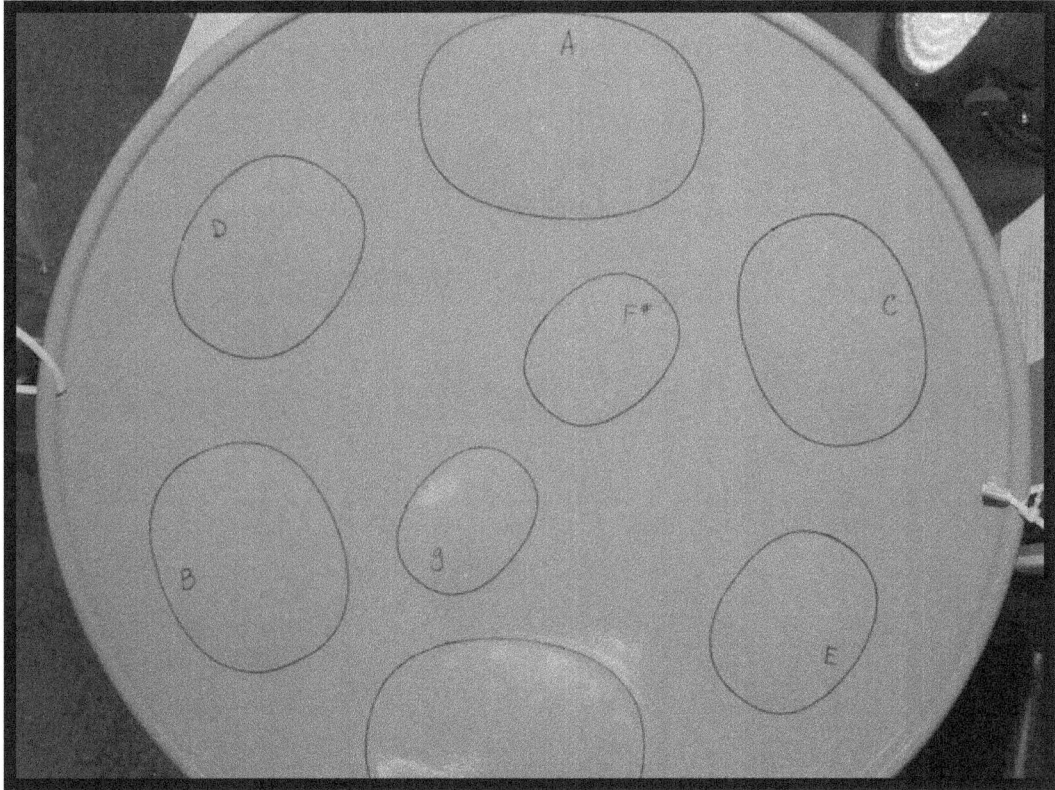

Anytime you strike the drums you have to be aware that you're creating a musical event. If you think of it as something more or less technical, you're thinking reductionistically.

Unknown

Age is an issue of mind over matter. If you don't mind, it doesn't matter. Unknown

I put an ad out looking for guitar and bass to play jazz. One of the people that responded was a young man just out of high school. He said he has always loved jazz.

Now, I'm pushing sixty and have played longer than this kid has been alive, but I was reminded by a close friend some many years ago that it's about the music.

The young man showed up, on time, with guitar and amp, song book and notebook. The kid could play. We added a bass player and off we went.

It's about the music!

Listen

I booked a gig, on a Saturday night, for an event at a local health club by their pool. A couple of my band mates then canceled due to unforeseen circumstances. So, I called a guy I know who had a calypso band and would fit in perfectly for the event. His band was very good having played together for many years.

Not wanting to miss this opportunity to play I said the only hitch was that I would be the percussion player. Jeff said OK, but they would still keep their regular percussion player.

I was a little disappointed but thought we could share the conga duties, and I wouldn't mind playing some percussion toys.

It was a beautiful night. We set up early, and Jeff gave me the set list for the night. As we started to play I realized I never did speak to the other percussionist about sharing so he just kept playing congas on all the songs. I got down on myself and a little mad. I started beating myself up for not communicating and not being able to play my congas.

After one song, toward the end of the first set, the veteran bass player yelled sternly to me, "HEY…LISTEN!"

"I'm sorry, what?" I questioned.

"You're not listening," he stated again, obviously miffed at what I was doing.

I then realized I was in my own little world and not even paying attention to the music. I thought playing with these guys would surely be an opportunity for me. Now I was leaving them with the impression I wasn't a very good player.

From that time on I've made it a focus to make sure I listen to what other musicians are playing. I can still hear that bass player's voice scolding me, "LISTEN!" when I catch myself drifting from the music.

I know the price of success:
dedication, hard work, and an
unremitting devotion to the
things you want to see happen.

R. L. Wright

The only time you run out of chances is when you stop taking them. Unknown

"You make the band?"

"Naw."

"You quitting?"

"Not yet."

To get your playing more forceful, hit the drums harder.

Keith Moon

Practice Right Unknown

I have been playing conga drums about a year. My teacher has given me a lot of rhythms so I can play many different styles of music. I'm not really good at playing any one of them though. One day I met another conga player named Brad.

"Hey, I hear you're a pretty good conga player," I state.

"Well, I've been playing twenty plus years, so I guess I should be. How long have you been playing?" Brad asks politely.

"I started about a year ago. I know a lot of different rhythms, but I don't think I'm getting any better," I explain.

Brad then asks, "How do you practice?"

"I practice almost every day for about an hour by going through all the rhythms I know for about three to five minutes each. So it takes me around an hour to play all the rhythms."

"I see, now I know why you are having problems. I want you to take one rhythm and play it and only it for one hour," instructs Brad.

"Seriously, that's a long time," I state.

"I know it is. You will find, though, that within that hour the rhythm will change. It will feel different and when it's right your hands will start putting in variations. It's nobody's fault; it just happens," Brad says with a smile like he has been in my same position. Then he continues, "There are all different levels of knowledge. You're at the first level being able to just remember and play a rhythm. After an hour of playing one rhythm you will be able to manipulate the rhythm and feel the rhythm not just with your head, but with your hands and body. This will give you a higher level of knowing."

"I'll give it a try,' I said. As a result I tried it and found out Brad was a smart guy who helped me improve. What a great gift to know there are many different ways to practice.

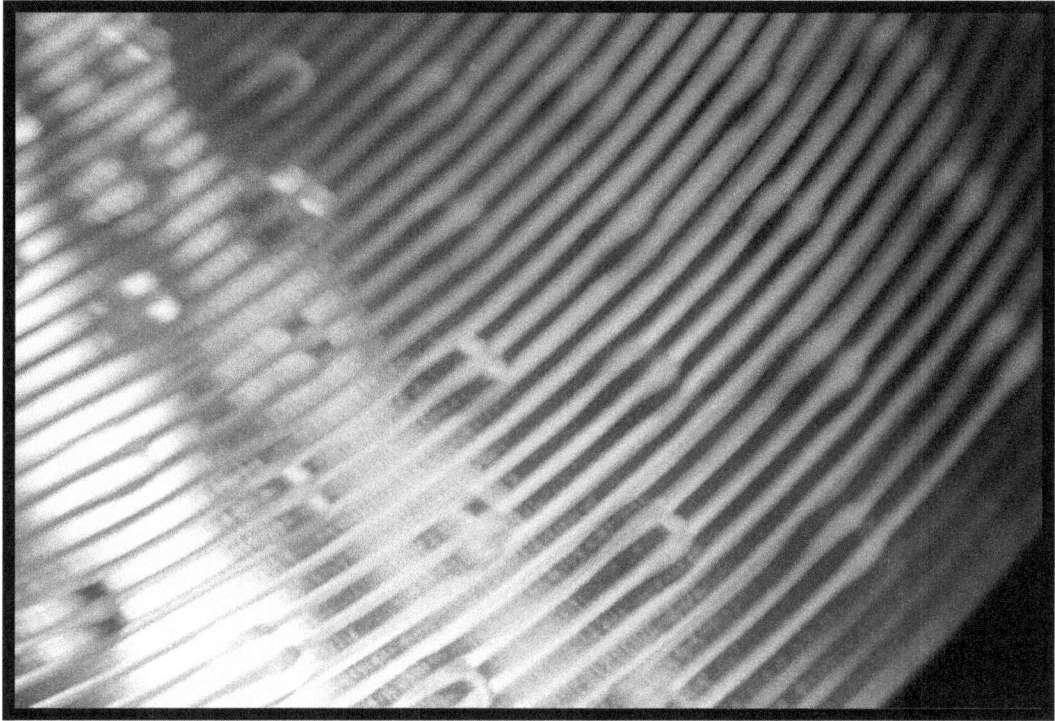

Everything has been thought of before, but the difficulty is to think of it again.

Goethe

Training deals not with an object but with the human spirit and human emotion.

B. Lee

A young drumming student is talking to his teacher at a practice session:

"I don't think I'm hitting them right."

"You're close with your technique, but you need more practice."

"What if I don't hit them right?"

"How do you feel when you play?"

"Sometimes I feel really good, and other times I think about technique 'cuz I don't think I sound as good."

"When you feel really good hold on to that, and don't worry so much about technique."

"But…"

"NO BUTS, look for that good feeling!"

Luck always seems against the man who depends on it.

Unknown

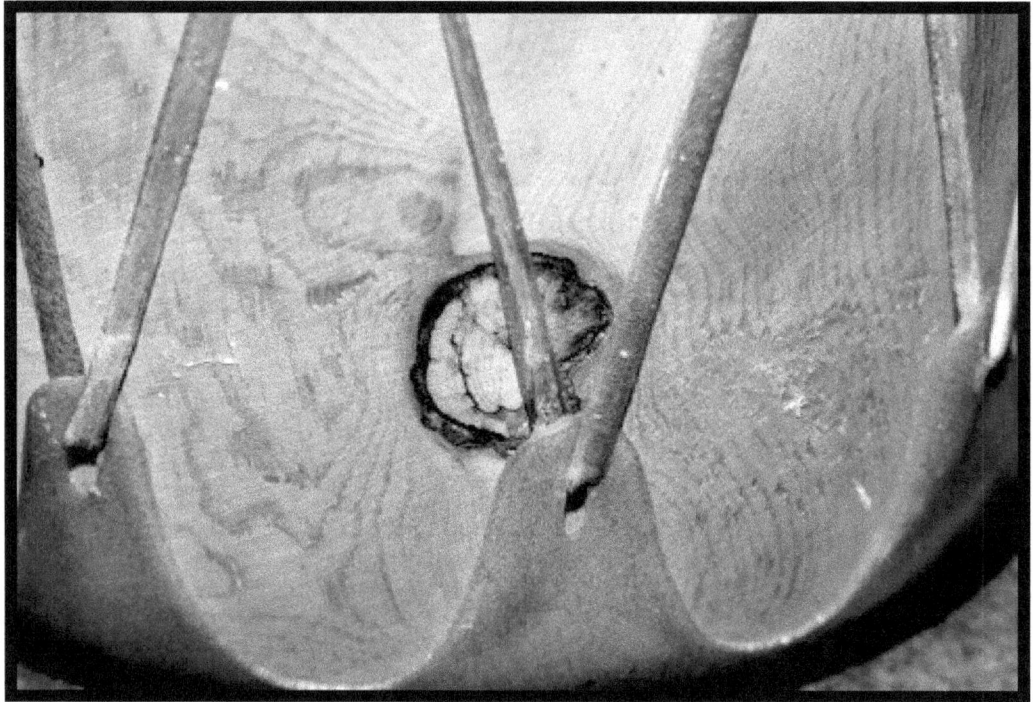

Do not be dependent upon others for your improvement. Pay your respects to the gods and buddhas, but never rely on them.

M. Miyamoto

Before receiving there must be giving.

Unknown

Make fear a friend Unknown

I was introduced to a guy who just started playing gigs. My friend that introduced us said he was having some problems and wanted to talk to me.

"So, what's on your mind?" I asked.

"Don't know if he told you, but I just started gigging in front of people."

"That's great. How can I help you?"

"Well… I'm getting so nervous. I get diarrhea before the gig. I start sweating like crazy and even shaking a bit. My stomach is a mess as well. It's throwing off my timing, and I'm not looking forward to playing."

"I see. Have you ever been in a performance situation like high school band, athletics, or theatre?"

"No, never!"

"I can tell you that every drummer or performer has been through the same thing to different degrees."

"What can I do? Can you help me?"

"I'll tell you this: the more you perform the more comfortable you'll become. The anxiety of performing may never go away, however, it will diminish. The second thing is to embrace your fear. Bring it close to you and know these feelings will come. Then, don't worry about them because you've embraced them. If you're sweating, then bring a small fan and set it up behind you."

"And this will work?"

"Not overnight, but yes I think this will help you."

"Thanks."

A mistake proves that someone stopped long enough to do something.

Unknown

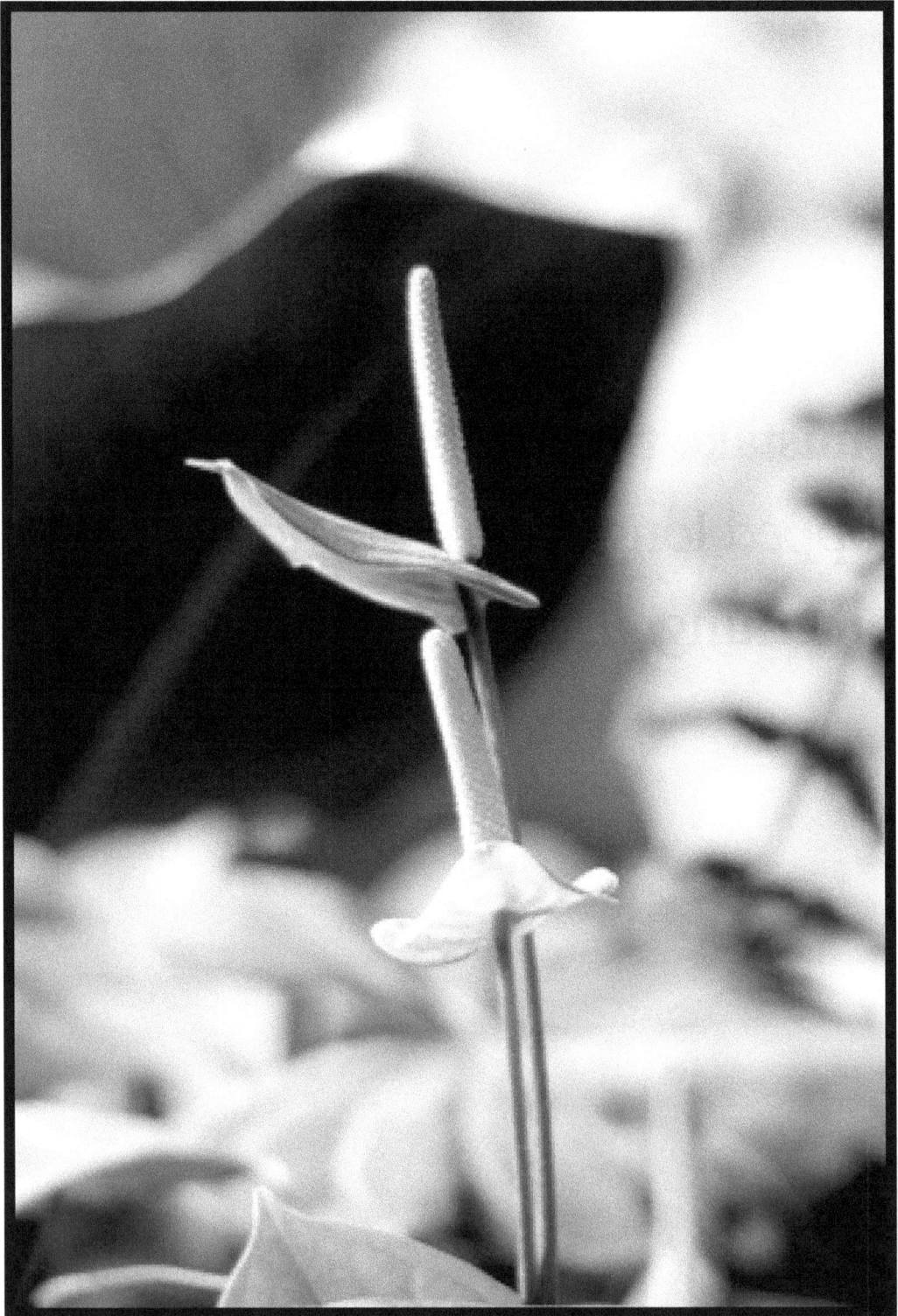

The more you do the more you are.

A Papadakis

A couple guys that drum are hanging around talking about the issue that most musicians have and that is how to go about getting gigs.

"I'm having trouble getting gigs."

"What kind of music do you play?"

"I only play rock."

"Oh, maybe if you worked on some grooves for different genres?"

"I like rock."

"Great, except, knowing other grooves will enable you to play with different bands and maybe play more gigs."

"Oh!"

Never take anything for granted.

B. Disraeli

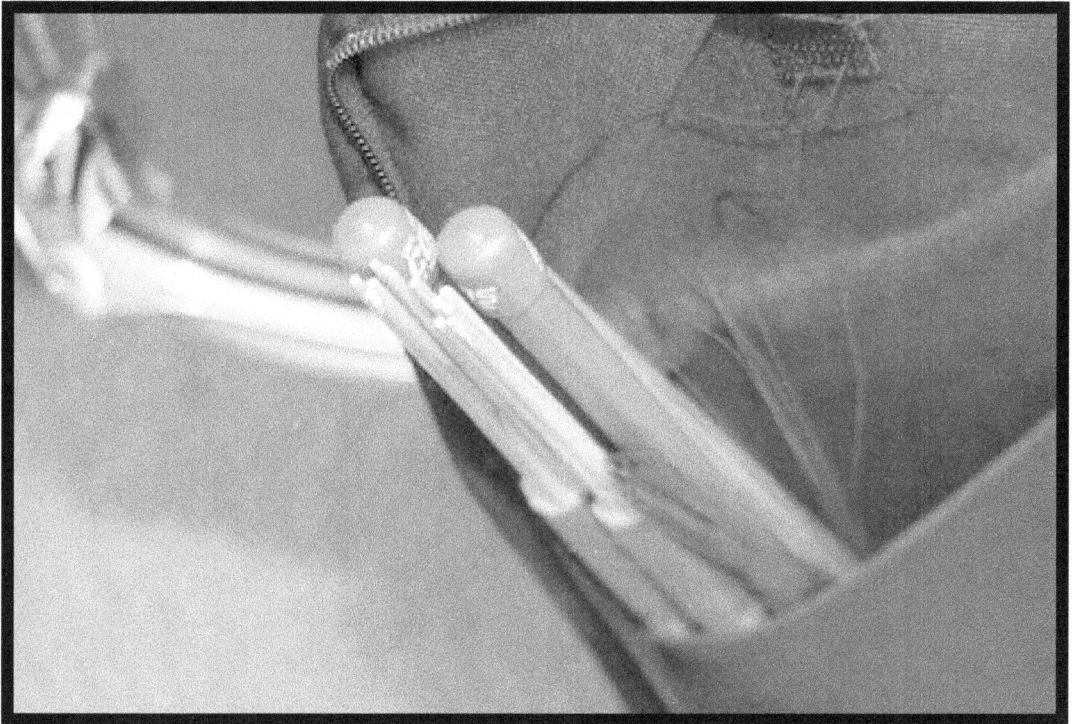

Everything that can be counted does not necessarily count; everything that counts cannot necessarily be counted. A. Einstein

Musicians talking during rehearsal.

"*Man*, I'm playing it correctly. Check the chart."

"Yeah, the right notes are there but…"

"But what?"

"How long have you been playing Latin music?"

"*Man*, what's that got to do with anything?"

"*Man*, EVERYTHING!"

But I think that any young drummer starting out today should get himself a great teacher and learn all there is to know about the instrument that he wants to play.

Buddy Rich

Everything I've ever done was out of fear of being mediocre.

Chet Atkins

A good groove releases adrenaline in your body. You feel uplifted, you feel centered, you feel calm and you feel powerful. You feel that energy. That's what good drumming is all about.

Mickey Hart

A band's only as good as its drummer.

Old Saying

Knowing others is wisdom; knowing yourself is enlightenment. Lao-Tzu

A student bought his first drum set from a second hand music store. The store also gave him a teacher recommendation. With the enthusiasm and excitement of a new adventure the student met with the teacher:

"I'd like to play like Buddy Rich, Steve Gadd or Dennis Chambers."

"Do you have that kind of talent?"

"I don't know, probably not."

"When you know what you have then you'll know what kind of drummer you can become."

"How do I discover that?"

"Practice and play, practice and play."

Make the metronome your friend,
not your enemy.

Vinnie Colaiuta

Change is not made without inconvenience, even from worse to better.

R. Hooker

I've been teaching drumming for a lot of years. It still amazes me when people sign up for lessons and say they've already been playing for a while. Some even say they are playing gigs.

When they arrive for their lesson I usually ask them to play something so I can get an idea of their technique and skill level. Afterwards, the conversation might go as follows:

"So, how long have you been playing?" I ask.

"A couple years," the student says.

"Where did you learn to play?"

"I taught myself. You know, just picked up things from YouTube, videos and the internet."

"Well, you've got some rhythm, but we'll have to work to change how you are playing."

"Really, cuz I thought I play just like_____."(insert famous drummer's name)

"You've picked up some bad habits to be honest. If you put in some work, practice, and commitment on your part I can help to move you closer to playing like_____."(insert same drummer's name)

"Cool, but I only want a couple of lessons."

After one, two, or even three lessons I can see the energy to change and improve is not something the student wants to give. The student stops taking lessons.

I often wonder if it's better to just imagine one is good rather than to expend the energy to become good.

Always desire to learn something useful.

Sophocles

Success is the place in the road where opportunity and preparation meet. Unknown

Phone rings:

"Hey, what's up?"

"You got anthing goin' tonight?"

"Naw, why?"

"Our drummer cancelled. Can you do the gig?"

"Uh, OK."

"Great, see you at 9:00 at Gibbys."

Later:

"Mom."

"Yes?"

"I got a problem."

"What is it?"

"I got asked to play a gig tonight."

"Oh, Honey, that's great!"

"Yeah, it should be, but I haven't been practicing, and it's a three hour gig."

"Oh my!"

"If I don't play well they'll never ask me again."

"Did you tell them you haven't been playing?"

"No, I was afraid."

"Maybe you should."

"Well…"

Do not consider painful what is good for you.

Euripedes

I hear and I forget.

I see and I remember.

I do and I understand.

Confucius

Example is not the main thing in influencing others. It is the only thing!

A. Schweitzer

Sometimes a majority simply means that all the fools are on the same side.

C. McDonald

When you know a thing to hold that you know it: and when you do not know a thing, to allow that you do not know it, this is knowledge.

Confucius

Everything has its' limits; iron ore cannot be educated into gold.

M. Twain

The way to bring out the best in you is not by chance. It is by preparation.

Unknown

If you play music with passion and love and honesty, then it will nourish your soul, heal your wounds and make your life worth living. Music is its own reward.

Sting

Music is not a matter of life or death...

It's much more important than that.

Unknown

One good thing about music,
when it hits you, you feel no pain.

Bob Marley

Russ "Rusito" Frost